THE WOLF EFFECT

THE WOLF EFFECT

EFFECT

A WILDERNESS REVIVAL STORY

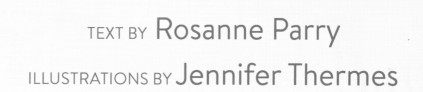

TEXT BY Rosanne Parry

ILLUSTRATIONS BY Jennifer Thermes

GREENWILLOW BOOKS

An Imprint of HarperCollinsPublishers

The Yellowstone region was first surveyed in 1870 by Nathaniel P. Langford and in 1871 by Ferdinand V. Hayden.

President Ulysses S. Grant created Yellowstone National Park on March 1, 1872.

LAMAR VALLEY
Human beings have lived here for at least eleven thousand years.

Road construction into the region began in the 1870s.

The Northern Pacific Railroad finished a line to the park in 1883.

This is Yellowstone National Park
Our nature preserve; our American ark.
A cradle of life, untrammeled and wild.
A haven for creatures, the fierce and the mild.

Indigenous Americans, prospectors, trappers, and settlers were removed from the park when it was formed.

But settlers began to raise cattle and sheep.
They cleared wolves from landscapes both level and steep.
Coyotes and bears all kill livestock the same,
But wolf packs alone took the worst of the blame.

Park rangers hunted the very last pack,

But afterwards, songbirds just didn't come back.

No slap of the beaver, no chirp of the sparrow;

The trees became scarce, and the streams became narrow.

So people decided
To bring the wolves home
To help mend the country
Where once they did roam.

These are the Rockies, their forests gone bare,
With only an echo of what once lived there.

These are the elk who hear the wolves' song,
Leaving the stream and moving along.
The song of the wolves, noses raised to the sky.
They howl as a pack with a fierce ancient cry.
It rings through the Rockies, their forests gone bare,
With only an echo of what once lived there.

But Bear, what if wolves kill *all* the elk?

Don't worry, they only take the old and sick ones.

What about my pups? Will wolves hunt us?

Coyote, old pal, nobody outlasts you. Mountain, desert, tundra, city—you are the master of migration. If I was a gambling bear, I'd bet all my pine nuts on you.

Wolves kill more elk than any other prey. Elk remain the most abundant large animal in the park. Wolves sometimes kill coyotes. Coyotes are the most adaptable predator in North America. They have never been endangered and can live in every ecosystem from urban to arctic.

Here are the willows that spring from the ground,
As soon as the trampling hooves aren't around.
The hooves of the elk who hear the wolves' song,
Leaving the stream and moving along.
The song of the wolves, noses raised to the sky.
They howl as a pack with a fierce ancient cry.
It rings through the Rockies, their forests gone bare,
With only an echo of what once lived there.

A variety of trees and shrubs, including willows, aspens, and cottonwoods, increased in number after the wolves moved the elk away from streams. These trees provide food for elk, moose, deer, and beavers. They also make a protective cover for animals who come to drink. Trees prevent erosion and they shade the water, making it easier for fish and amphibians to survive.

Bear! Where did all these trees come from?

Don't know. Don't care. I'm just enjoying a nap in the shade!

Here are the beavers who dam up the creek,
Giving water and shelter to all those who seek.
The water feeds willows that spring from the ground,
As soon as the trampling hooves aren't around,
The hooves of the elk who hear the wolves' song,
Leaving the stream and moving along.
The song of the wolves, noses raised to the sky.
They howl as a pack with a fierce ancient cry.
It rings through the Rockies, their forests gone bare,
With only an echo of what once lived there.

How can you sleep, Bear? Do you hear those frogs! Can you see the fish?

Umph!

Do you smell that? Rabbits!

Since the wolves returned, beaver populations have increased in Yellowstone. Their ponds provide habitat for insects, fish, birds, amphibians, and small mammals. The ponds feed the aquifer that makes the whole region more resistant to drought and also less vulnerable to wildfires.

The pond shelters songbirds, the warblers, the lark,
Whose music now echoes across the whole park.
The park where the beavers build dams on the creek,
to give water and shelter to all those who seek.
The water feeds willows that spring from the ground,
As soon as the trampling hooves aren't around,
The hooves of the elk who hear the wolves' song,
Leaving the stream and moving along.
The song of the wolves, noses raised to the sky.
They howl as a pack with a fierce ancient cry.
It rings through the Rockies that wolves helped revive.
Where forests and creatures and people now thrive.

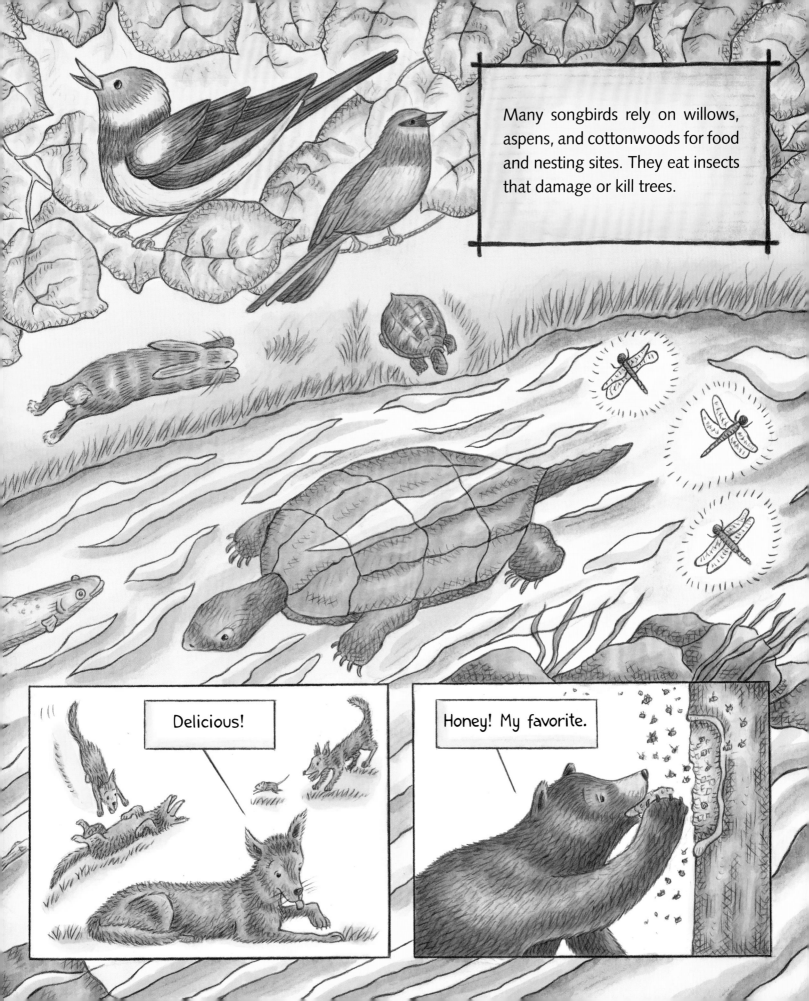

Many songbirds rely on willows, aspens, and cottonwoods for food and nesting sites. They eat insects that damage or kill trees.

Delicious!

Honey! My favorite.

So the park that was wild became wilder still
More life, more abundance on valley and hill.
The wolves touched off a cascade of good things
From drought resistance to butterfly wings.

Wolves changed the ecosystem of Yellowstone in far-reaching ways. These changes are called a trophic cascade. They will help Yellowstone Park meet the challenges of climate change with greater resilience.

Here are some of the animals who benefit from the wolf effect.
Can you find them all in the pages of this book?

Beaver

Black Bear

Bison

Cougar

Coyote

Elk

Golden Eagle

Great Gray Owl

Pine Marten

Porcupine

Raccoon

Raven

Red Fox

Skunk

Snapping Turtle

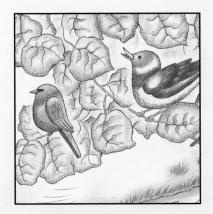

Songbirds

White-Tailed Deer

White-Tailed Jackrabbit

A Brief History of Wolves in the American West

The earliest wolves of North America were dire wolves. They were larger than gray wolves and they hunted camels, saber-toothed cats, mammoths, and mastodons. Like their oversized prey, dire wolves did not survive the Ice Age. But a new wolf came to North America from Eurasia, a species that is the direct ancestor of today's gray wolves. These wolves were smaller and more adaptable than the dire wolf. They spread to every ecosystem on the continent.

Gray wolves lived alongside Indigenous North Americans, who held them in great respect. When North America was settled by people from other countries, they brought with them a much different perception of wolves. They felt it was their duty to rid the continent of a dangerous predator. As settlers moved from the East Coast to the West, wolves were shot, poisoned, and trapped by the thousands. In response, the few surviving wolves became wary of humans and retreated into the most wild and remote wilderness areas.

Many settlers believed there was no end to the wilderness, but by the late 1800s, people were beginning to understand the need for conservation. They saw that uncontrolled logging, mining, farming, and urban development polluted the water and the air and made wildfires, floods, and landslides more common. They understood that wild places were vital to human well-being and could be lost forever.

Yellowstone National Park was created in 1872 by President Ulysses S. Grant. It is America's oldest national park. Yellowstone covers 3,472 square miles. It is high in the Rocky Mountains and is part of the largest intact temperate and subalpine forest ecosystem in the world.

Once Yellowstone Park was established, an army garrison was built, and the soldiers drove Native Americans, settlers, trappers, and prospectors out. Wolves who unknowingly left the park to hunt on the surrounding ranches were shot. Park rangers killed Yellowstone's remaining wolves between 1914 and 1926.

With no wolves to hunt them, the elk population grew. They ate up not just the grasses but also the shrubs and sapling trees that kept the ecosystem healthy. Dozens of mammals and birds who relied on those plants for shelter and food declined in number or disappeared. The lack of trees to stabilize stream banks and provide shade destroyed fish habitats. Without numerous beaver ponds to refresh the aquifer, the whole region became more vulnerable to drought and wildfire. Wolf populations continued to plummet across the West due to loss of prey and habitat, and from campaigns of extermination. In 1974, gray wolves were listed under the Endangered Species Act.

In the early 1990s, people began to work toward the reintroduction of wolves to Yellowstone Park. In 1995, the first packs of wolves were brought to the

park from Canada. Each pack was kept in a large pen for a few months to get them used to the area. When the pens were opened, the wolves quickly found territories with good den sites and abundant prey. Because Yellowstone is not fenced in, the wolves do sometimes wander out of the park, but most of the packs find everything they need to survive within its boundaries.

The Yellowstone wolves continue to thrive, decades after their reintroduction. They attract thousands of eager wolf watchers to the park every year. They are the most closely studied wolves in the world. Biologists are seeing a trophic cascade—the wolf effect—that exceeds every expectation. Both elk and coyote populations have dropped back to healthy levels while hundreds of plant and animal species have flourished.

In 2020, gray wolves were removed from the endangered species list, making it legal to hunt them again. Hundreds of wolves have been killed in the years since. Conversations about how to best coexist with wolves are sure to continue for many years to come.

—*Rosanne Parry*

Artist's Note

When creating the art for a picture book, I always look for exciting visual ways to capture the feeling of the story. Conveying the essence of an event—as was done in the spread illustrating the actual return of wolves to Yellowstone—rather than portraying it with technical perfection can often speak more clearly to a reader. The meaning is there, enhanced by the color, mood, movement, and emotion in the artwork. My hope is that the reader will be excited to keep turning the pages to see what happens next.

A note regarding the panels depicting railroad laborers—while it could not be confirmed for certain whether Chinese immigrants worked on the Yellowstone branch of tracks, such workers were essential to the construction of railroads across the western United States, which in turn provided access to the park.

It was a great joy to spend time learning about and drawing wolves for this book. May many more people celebrate and appreciate these magnificent creatures!

—*Jennifer Thermes*

Glossary

aquifer: An underground area of rock and/or sediment that holds water.

carrion: The decaying flesh of a dead animal. Many animals, such as coyotes and crows, eat carrion.

drought: A period of time without enough rain or snowfall to provide for the water needs of an ecosystem.

ecosystem: An interconnected community of animals and plants living together in an environment.

endangered species: An animal or plant in danger of disappearing from the earth entirely and becoming extinct.

erosion: When small pieces of soil or rock are worn away and moved by water or wind from one place to another.

haven: A safe place.

livestock: Farm animals, such as cows, goats, and sheep, that provide a product, such as milk or wool.

migration: The movement of animals from one place to another in response to a change of season or a need for resources such as food or water.

nature preserve: Land protected from development and set aside for the preservation of animals and plants and the public's enjoyment.

predator: An animal that hunts and eats other animals.

prey: An animal that is hunted by another animal for food.

prospectors: People who dig in the earth for mineral resources such as gold, silver, or oil.

resilience: The ability to successfully cope with changes and disturbances and continue to thrive.

Rockies: The Rocky Mountains, also called the Rockies, stretch 3,000 miles, from Canada to New Mexico, and are the largest mountain range in North America.

survey: To write down the form, features, and position of land using careful measurements.

trophic cascade: A series of changes that can occur in an ecosystem's food web, such as when the behavior of a predator (such as a wolf) impacts the population of a prey animal (such as an elk), potentially benefiting other animals and plants.

untrammeled: Not confined, restricted, or limited.

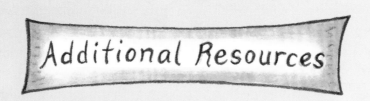

Additional Resources

FOR YOUNG READERS

American Museum of Natural History. *Wolf Pups Join the Pack*. New York: Union Square Kids, 2017.

Gyetxw, Hetxw'ms (Brett D. Huson), and Natasha Donovan, illus. *The Wolf Mother*. Winnipeg: HighWater Press, 2021

Pringle, Laurence, and Meryl Henderson, illus. *Wolves! Strange and Wonderful*. New York: Astra Young Readers, 2022.

National Park Service: Yellowstone National Park Sound Library: www.nps.gov/yell/learn/photosmultimedia/soundlibrary.htm

FOR ADULT READERS

Smith, Douglas W., Daniel R. Stahler, and Daniel R. MacNulty, eds. Foreword by Jane Goodall. *Yellowstone Wolves: Science and Discovery in the World's First National Park*. Chicago: University of Chicago Press, 2020.

*For every child with a heart
for the wilderness, a head for science,
and a voice for change—R. P.*

For Jeremy and Emily—J. T.

The Wolf Effect: A Wilderness Revival Story. Text copyright © 2024 by Rosanne Parry. Illustrations copyright © 2024 by Jennifer Thermes. All rights reserved. Manufactured in Italy. For information address HarperCollins Children's Books, a division of HarperCollins Publishers, 195 Broadway, New York, NY 10007. www.harpercollinschildrens.com The illustrations in this book were created using watercolor and colored pencil on Arches hot pressed paper. The text type is Times Europa and Syntax LT Std.

Library of Congress Cataloging-in-Publication Data

Names: Parry, Rosanne, author. I Thermes, Jennifer, illustrator. Title: The wolf effect : a wilderness revival story / by Rosanne Parry ; illustrated by Jennifer Thermes.
Description: First edition. I New York, NY : Greenwillow Books, an imprint of HarperCollins Publishers, 2024. I Includes bibliographical references. I Audience: Ages 4–8 I Audience: Grades 2–3 I Summary: "An exploration of the reintroduction of wolves into Yellowstone Park, and the positive cascade effect they caused on its environment and surroundings"— Provided by publisher.

Identifiers: LCCN 2023031724 I ISBN 9780062969583 (hardcover) Subjects: LCSH: Gray wolf—Yellowstone National Park—Juvenile literature.I Gray wolf—Reintroduction—Yellowstone National Park—Juvenile literature. I Gray wolf—Ecology—Yellowstone National Park—Juvenile literature. I Endangered species—Conservation—Yellowstone National Park—Juvenile literature. I Ecology—Yellowstone National Park—Juvenile literature. I Yellowstone National Park—Juvenile literature.
Classification: LCC QL737.C22 P373 2024 I DDC 599.773—dc23/eng/20230912
LC record available at https://lccn.loc.gov/2023031724

24 25 26 27 28 RTLO 10 9 8 7 6 5 4 3 2 1   First Edition

 Greenwillow Books